GERMAN BOMBERS OVER RUSSIA

The small size Geschwader identity code, S7, has been painted over a former identity on this Ju 87D-5 of I/StG 3. Fuselage band is yellow (726/223/3a).

BRYAN PHILPOTT

GERMAN BOMBERS OVER RUSSIA

WORLD WAR 2 PHOTO ALBUM NUMBER 8

A selection of German wartime photographs
from the Bundesarchiv, Koblenz

PSL Patrick Stephens, Cambridge

First published in 1979

British Library Cataloguing in Publication Data

German bombers over Russia. – (World War 2 photo album; 8).
  1. World War, 1939–1945 – Aerial operations, German – Pictorial works
  2. World War, 1939–1945 – Campaigns – Russia – Pictorial works
  3. Bombers – History – Pictorial works
  I. Philpott, Bryan   II. Bundesarchiv
  III. Series

940.54'21   D787

ISBN 0 85059 346 8 (Casebound)
ISBN 0 85059 337 9 (Softbound)

Photoset in 10pt Plantin Roman. Printed in Great Britain on 100 gsm Pedigree coated cartridge and bound by The Garden City Press Limited, Letchworth, Hertfordshire SG6 1JS, for the publishers, Patrick Stephens Limited, Bar Hill, Cambridge, CB3 8EL.

CONTENTS

Acknowledgements
The author and publisher would like to express their sincere thanks to Dr Matthias Haupt and Herr Meinrad Nilges of the Bundesarchiv for their assistance, without which this book would have been impossible.

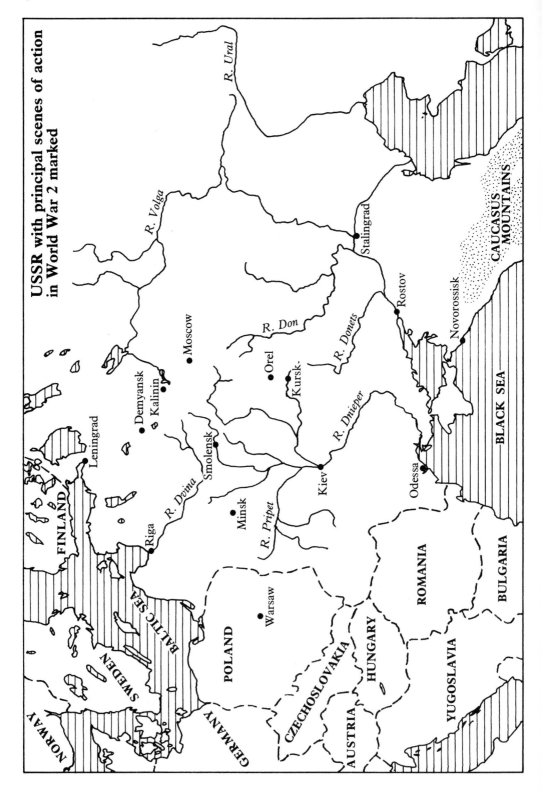

USSR with principal scenes of action in World War 2 marked

AUTHOR'S INTRODUCTION

From the early 1920s Hitler considered Russia to be Germany's prime enemy. However, he could do little to secure the land he needed to create *Lebensraum* (living space), for his new Germany, until such time as his forces were strong enough to overcome the numerically superior, but poorly equipped Soviet army and air force.

To offer some form of security to his eastern boundaries, Hitler entered into a Russo-German pact in 1939; an agreement he had no intention of honouring, but one which would give him time to plan what he expected to be a successful onslaught on an unsuspecting ally.

Despite mounting misgivings among the German General Staff, Hitler started to make his invasion plans as early as October 1940, the basis of these being the establishment in occupied Poland of airfields, refuelling bases and fuel dumps.

The General Staff feared a war on two fronts as they realised that this was beyond their capabilities, but such was Hitler's obsession to crush Communism that he would not listen to reason. Hermann Goering tried desperately to sway the Führer from his plan but, by the autumn of 1940 when the Luftwaffe chiefs were advised of the proposed operation against Russia, he appeared to have abandoned his attempts and predictably sided with Hitler. A firm indication of his change in attitude came when Generaloberst Alfred Keller – the commander of Luftflotte 1 whose task was the assault on Leningrad – remarked that Germany had a treaty with Russia, only to be told by Goering not to worry about politics and to leave that to the Führer. With hindsight it is easy to see that a move against Russia, while Britain remained undefeated in the west, although bringing fresh glories to Germany in the short term, was ultimately to lead to defeat.

Hampered by bad weather the Luftwaffe moved men, materials and aircraft to airfields from which they could mount 'Operation Barbarossa', the code name for the invasion of Russia. The security measures undertaken were such that very few people apart from those directly concerned were aware of the build-up of forces which began in earnest in early June, already a delay of three weeks caused by a very late thaw. Nearly two-thirds of the Luftwaffe's total front-line strength was moved into position ready for the assault; units came from the Mediterranean, France, and Germany, leaving these areas somewhat denuded, but without any real likelihood of coming under attack from the western powers.

Prior to the Russian assault Luftwaffe and army chiefs had argued about the tactics to be used. The army wanted to mount a dawn attack against Russian troop concentrations, but needed assurance of complete air cover to protect them from the Soviet air force. The Luftwaffe pointed out that the best policy was to destroy Russian aircraft on the ground, but if they delayed their attacks until dawn it would be a full hour before they could reach the forward enemy bases, by which time news of the invasion would have caused the fighters to be dispersed. There seemed to be little chance of compromise, since the army pointed out that, if the Luftwaffe crossed the front in darkness to be in position to attack Russian bases when the ground forces opened their assault, their passing over the Russian border might well alert the defenders. In the end it was decided that hand-picked crews – experienced men with many hours of blind-flying behind them – would take off early, climb to high altitude before crossing the Russian frontier, and open the attack at precisely 0315 hours.

On the morning of June 22 He 111s of KG 53 and Ju 88s of KG 3, both units from FlKps II of Kesselring's Luftflotte 2, left their bases to put this plan into action. Soviet forward bases had all been well reconnoitred and pin-pointed by Oberst Rowehl's Aufklärungsgruppen, and it was these airfields where personnel were to have their Sunday morning rudely awakened by the advance guard of the Luftwaffe. Almost at the same time as the He 111s and Ju 88s struck, large formations of Ju 87s, Do 17s, Bf 109s and Bf 110s crossed the frontier in support of the army, and met virtually no aerial opposition. The Russian air force was numerically twice the size of the Luftwaffe, but it was in the process of changing to more modern aircraft, and on many airfields both old and new were lined up in neat uncamouflaged rows. Early in the morning of June 22 Stalin had, in fact, been made aware that a German attack was imminent. He had tried to warn his military commanders but his message to disperse troops and aircraft was delayed in the Soviet communication network.

Luftwaffe bombers involved in the opening attacks used a new type of fragmentation bomb known as the SD 2. This was a three-inch diameter cylindrical weapon weighing 4 lb, and carried in containers of various capacities depending on the aircraft involved. Machines such as the Ju 88 and He 111 could carry 360 SD 2s while Ju 87s and Bf 109s managed 96. The bombs were dropped in rapid succession and, after release from the aircraft, opened to form a pair of wings which rotated them to the ground where they exploded on impact. Dispersion over a large area was practically guaranteed by the method of delivery, and the shrapnel generated by the explosion was very effective against parked aircraft, soft-skinned vehicles and troops. But there was a disadvantage both with the SD 2 and its 20 lb brother the SD 10; they were liable to 'hold-up' in the bomber and, with live fuses, likely to explode tearing holes in the aircraft's skin, or even totally destroying it. On June 22, there were several reports of Ju 88s and Do 17s folding up for no apparent reason. The absence of flak and Russian fighters quickly pin-pointed the problems to be SD 10 bombs which had failed to leave the aircraft.

As a result Kesselring banned horizontal bombers from carrying either SD 2 or SD 10 fragmentation weapons and these were eventually limited to Ju 87s and Hs 123s which carried them on wing racks where they could be clearly seen if they failed to release. In fact, the SD 2 bomb had a very short life in the Russian campaign as far as horizontal bombers were concerned because, as the war progressed and the Russian defences became more effective forcing the bombers to seek the sanctuary of greater altitude, they could not be used from jettisonable containers, and were therefore confined solely to the low-level ground-support aircraft.

The element of total surprise, outstanding planning, superior equipment, and the will to push home their advantages gave the German bomber crews an opening to the Russian campaign they could hardly have believed possible. By the end of the day on June 22 the Luftwaffe had recorded the single biggest daily destruction of an opposing air force. A total of 1,811 Russian aircraft lay in ruins and, of these, 1,489 were destroyed on their own airfields; on the debit side the Germans lost 35 aircraft. The reports from the front were so incredible that even Goering found them hard to believe and ordered checks to be carried out in the field.

A Luftwaffe total force of 2,770 aircraft, of which 1,945 had been serviceable for operations on the morning of June 22, could look back on a day's work which, after the war, would be confirmed in the official Soviet publication *History of the Great Patriotic War of the Soviet Union*, with some pride. But their efforts did not have a long-term effect on the Soviet war machine. Production of replacement aircraft was not adversely affected as the Germans did not have a strategic bombing policy and, even if they had, they had no aeroplanes capable of carrying it out. Consequently, production of aircraft for the Soviet air force continued to gather pace at factories in the Urals which were well beyond the reach of the bombers then forming the backbone of the Kampfgeschwadern on the Russian front. The destruction of aircraft was a serious problem for the Russians for a short period of time. However, by virtue of the fact that the vast majority of these had occurred on the ground, losses of trained crews had not reached anything like the same proportions. The result was that, as new aircraft reached the squadrons, trained men were available to take them into action immediately.

With the Soviet air force rendered temporarily impotent the Luftwaffe bombers reverted to their normal task of supporting the army in a tactical role. Dive bombers and fighter bombers acted in the close support role, while level bombers like the Ju 88 and He 111 devoted their efforts to communications, troop concentrations and targets which were aimed at clearing the way for the army advance. One of the main strengths of the Luftwaffe at this time was its reconnaissance units. The efficiency of the crews and the number of aircraft operating enabled army and Luftwaffe commanders quickly to obtain details of Russian build-ups. They could then take the necessary action either with quick strikes by Ju 87s, fighter bombers, or the heavier twins. One lesson they did not learn from the activities of the reconnaissance units was the fortitude of the infantry man they were up against. Instead of running for cover on the appearance of enemy aircraft, the Russian soldier stood his ground and fired back with any available weapon. Losses in reconnaissance aircraft were high, and similarly bombers also suffered when they made low-level attacks; the latter gradually grew to serious proportions and by September 1941 the Luftwaffe had lost 1,603 aircraft with a further 1,028 damaged. Such was the euphoria of success that insufficient attention was paid to these losses until it was too late.

Throughout the summer and autumn the victorious German forces advanced deeper and deeper into Russia, stretching their all-important supply lines to lengths which started to prove problematic as far as the Luftwaffe transport units were concerned. Bombers continued to support the army with Ju 87s, which were now present in ever-increasing numbers, causing difficulties to Russian troops and armour whenever they encountered them. On the Russian front the Ju 87 was able to come into its own simply because for most of the time it was able to operate in areas where its own fighters held complete air superiority. Russian I–153s, I–15s, Ratas and Curtiss P40s were no match for the escorting Bf 109s whose pilots had little difficulty in reaching *experten* (ace) status after a good day's operations. Later, aircraft like the MiG 3 and Yak 1 caused greater problems, but in the first six months of the campaign the Luftwaffe virtually had complete control of the skies. While the dive-bombers acted in close support roles the heavies were often called upon to remove stronger pockets of resistance. One such occasion occurred on June 28 when General Heinz Guderian's Panzer Group 2 was held up by the fortress of Brest-Litovsk. Despite repeated attacks by Ju 87s the walls remained intact; so seven Ju 88A-4s of KG 3 were detailed to attack using 3,500 lb bombs. Heavy fire from the defenders seriously upset the bombing runs of the Ju 88s but two of them managed direct hits on the walls of the fortress which capitulated the following morning.

The German thrust into Russia continued at a fast pace with air support being a vital ingredient, and the blitzkrieg technique to which General von Richthofen's F1Kps VIII Ju 87s had contributed a great deal, proving an invaluable weapon when pockets of armour and stubborn infantry were encountered.

By the end of September Leningrad was under siege and the army was within 290 miles of Moscow; 665,000 Russian troops – about one-third of those available at the outbreak of Operation Barbarossa – had been killed or captured, most of these in the battles for Uman and Kiev which were now both in German hands. At this time it looked as though Hitler's prophesy of a short war leading to an easy victory was coming true. But there were factors which had not been taken into account, and were now beginning to have a telling effect.

Losses of aircraft in the Kampfgeschwadern and Stukageschwadern were becoming serious, with few replacements reaching the front-line units; the onset of a severe winter brought problems which neither the Luftwaffe nor army could overcome with the equipment available, and morale was beginning to falter.

On October 1 the drive against Moscow began. Since July it had been a major target for Luftwaffe bombers, which due to indifferent leadership and poor planning, had caused little damage to the Russian capital. In early July Hitler had resolved that Goering's bombers would raze Leningrad and Moscow to the ground, but by the 15th of the month nothing had happened and the Führer was forced into goading Goering to send his bombers into the attack. The importance of Moscow, both as a political seat and as the centre of military planning and communications, should have put it at the top of the Luftwaffe's strategic targets from the opening of the campaign. The fact that it was not simply underlines once again that the Luftwaffe was not geared to operate in a strategic role. Absence of a central policy-making command was never more apparent than in the Russian campaign, where time and again individual army commanders were able to insist on tactical help from widely dispersed bomber units which themselves were part of separately commanded air forces, instead of a centrally controlled and directed command such as that operated by the RAF.

On July 22 a total of 127 bombers comprising Ju 88s from KGs 3 and 54, He 111s from KGs 53 and 55, supported by KG 28's two pathfinder Gruppen, Kampfgruppe 100 and III/KG 26, dropped over 100 tons of bombs on Moscow, but these and the 50,000 incendiaries failed to cause very much concern or damage. The Kremlin, which had been the target of II/KG 55, was hit several times but the incendiaries failed to penetrate the extremely strong structure. The following night 115 bombers returned, and the night after 100 skirted the vast quantity of searchlights and effective anti-aircraft fire – which many veteran bomber crews claimed was as good as London's at the height of the Blitz – but again achieved little. From then on the intensity of the raids decreased with alarming speed until only three or four bombers per night were being sent to the target. Of the 76 raids carried out against Moscow in 1941, 59 of them involved less than ten aircraft. The result of this puny attempt not surprisingly caused many questions to be asked about the effectiveness of the bomber force; the answer seems to have been that it was more effective as a tactical support weapon in the battlefield.

Oddly enough, in September 1941, the Luftwaffe carried out a week's strategic bombing campaign against the Red Fleet, the aircraft used being Ju 87s of StG 2 which were more suited to a tactical role. None the less Oberstleutnant Dinort's I and III StG 2, which were part of von Richthofen's F1Kps VIII attached to Luftflotte 2, took off from Tyrkovo on the morning of September 23 to open their campaign against the Russian Fleet which threatened the flow of raw materials from Sweden as well as supplies to Finland and the Baltic ports. The Ju 87s flew very high to avoid the Russian anti-aircraft defences; consequently, they were faced with a dive from 15,000 to 4,000 feet when they reached the target area. The accuracy of bombing by these highly skilled experts soon accounted for many small vessels as well as the 23,600-ton battleship *Marat*, the decisive blow against the latter being achieved by Oberleutnant Hans-Ulrich Rudel, who was later to become the most decorated Ju 87 pilot for his work against Russian armour.

On the afternoon of September 23 the Ju 87s returned, establishing a pattern they were to follow until the 28th. During this time they suffered heavy losses, among them being Hauptmann Steen the popular III Gruppe commander, but they caused inestimable damage to the fleet and the anchorage at Kronstadt. The Ju 87s were all that the Luftwaffe had in sufficient quantity to carry out a campaign of this nature. Although far from ideal for the task, they achieved what they had set out to do, but had hardly had

time to take stock of their situation before being moved to the central front to assist in the siege of Kiev.

The front along which the Germans were committed was over 2,000 miles long, stretching from the North Cape to the Black Sea. To keep army units supported with equipment and help them tactically meant that there was a continuous 'juggling' of units which in the long run was doomed to failure.

Requests from army commanders for air support gradually increased to a degree where the Luftwaffe bomber force was nothing more than airborne artillery. In the battle which raged around Kiev, German bombers achieved some success in blockading the battlefield thus denying supplies to the Russian troops, this being achieved by concentrating solely on communication systems. For a month Ju 88s, He 111s and Do 17s systematically attacked railway installations, bridges, trains and viaducts, achieving short-term objectives in the disruption of supplies, but nothing in the way of a longterm strategic advantage. To have reached the latter would have meant concentration on major junctions, marshalling yards and rail centres, but the Kampfgeschwadern had neither the weapons capable of creating a long-term knock-out blow nor the aircraft to deliver it. The result was that the 6,000 sorties flown against railway targets in the first six months of the Russian campaign caused an average disruption to the Russians of less than six hours.

The autumn rains turned roads and airfields into quagmires; aircraft became bogged down and the German army slithered to a halt 19 miles from Moscow. When the rain turned to snow and the Russian winter set in, problems increased by the hour. As far as the Luftwaffe was concerned, they were not equipped to withstand such extremes of temperature and conditions. There was no proper winter clothing for air or ground crews, no special cold weather equipment for the aircraft, and spares were at a premium. At night temperatures fell to below minus 20° F and crews had to get up to run engines, shovel snow away from the aircraft, and check guns and bomb release mechanisms. Some of the more delicate tasks related to the checking of equipment could not be carried out wearing thick gloves, so frostbite became another hazard which had to be faced. Added to these problems was the one of morale;

conditions did not of course help this, but neither did the fact that most units had been fighting continuously for six months and crews were desperately in need of a break away from the front line.

Since the end of October there had been ominous signs that front-line units needed re-equipping and rest; serviceability rates began to fall and with them the ability of the bomber units to provide the support they had done in the past. This state of affairs was not really surprising as, since June, combat units of the Luftwaffe had been involved in operations almost every day, the dive-bomber Gruppen achieving a daily sortie rate of 75 per cent of their available aircraft and the level bombers 40 per cent. A truly remarkable achievement and one which contributed a great deal to the success of Operation Barbarossa.

In late November, what was to prove the final phase of Operation Taifun (the drive against Moscow) began, and it was then that some of the first signs of the strain on the Luftwaffe began to show. Reconnaissance reports indicated that large-scale transport movements were converging on Moscow from the east, but no action was taken by any of the Kampfgeschwadern in the area. This was a mistake admitted to after the war by Kesselring who, in a letter to a friend, stated that the significance of the movements was not appreciated. It seems more likely that the units concerned could not have mounted a worthwhile strike even if they had wanted to, due to the low serviceability and lack of supplies.

By the end of 1941 Luftwaffe aircraft strength on the Eastern Front had fallen to 1,700 aircraft, and these were hard-pressed to give sufficient support to avoid a total collapse along the 2,000-mile front.

On December 5 the Russians mounted a major counter-offensive and this came at a time when Kesselring's Luftflotte 2 and FlKps II had been transferred to the Mediterranean. This move was planned since October but occurred at a time when several other units were in Germany being re-equipped with new aircraft and replacement personnel.

To the Germans it seemed incredible that the Russians were capable of mounting and supporting a large-scale offensive. Intelligence had reported success after success, since June 1941, with over 1½ million men killed or taken prisoner, and over 15,000

aircraft destroyed. These claims were later somewhat reduced but even so the losses were quite staggering.

None the less, during the following three months the German army was pushed back on all fronts until the first Russian offensive petered out in March 1942. What the Germans should have appreciated was that, although their successes on the battlefield were considerable, the absence of a strategic bombing programme or aircraft of sufficient range to carry out such a campaign, enabled factories well beyond the reach of medium bombers to produce far more tanks, aircraft and arms than were being lost. Similarly, training establishments were able to continue unhindered in much the same way as the Allies' Empire Air Training Scheme in Australia, Canada, the USA and South Africa. The flow of new equipment, and more importantly trained personnel, was something that the Luftwaffe was not able to enjoy to the same degree as its opponents.

The vast wealth of raw materials available to Russian industry was also unmolested, and their supplies of fuel oil and lines of communication never came under serious threat. A strategic bombing campaign against such targets would undoubtedly have brought a different end to the Russian campaign. As it was, in 1942 Hitler looked to new areas where he could strike at the Russians in depth, and his attention focused on the oilfields of the Caucasus.

The complex army plans around which the new spring offensive pivoted cannot be covered in any depth in this narrative, but they all relied on air support which again was predominantly in the tactical role.

To the forefront once again was von Richthofen's FlKps VIII, now part of Luftflotte 4, whose main task was to give support in the Crimea. During the raids on Sevastopol, which started on June 2, bombers from FlKps VIII – which now included the much-improved Ju 87D – averaged 600 sorties per day during which they dropped 2,500 tons on the beleaguered city, and this rate of air bombardment was supported by artillery until the Russians surrendered on July 4. The fortress of Sevastopol proved a tougher nut to crack than anticipated by the German planners, who had allowed five days for it to be brought to its knees. It took five weeks; one of the many examples of over-confidence which come to light when the Russian campaign is studied in depth. One of the major pockets of resistance encountered during the five weeks' siege was a raft containing 164 anti-aircraft guns. This was anchored in Severnaya Bay where it commanded a large area of air, land and sea approaches.

On June 25 it was decided that I/KG 51 should have another crack at removing this thorn in the Luftwaffe's side, and two Ju 88A–4s piloted by Hauptmann Fuhrhop, the Staffelkapitan of the 2nd Staffel, and Oberleutnant Hinrichs, both of whom had made three previous attacks, were assigned the task. The plan was for Hinrichs to suppress the flak while the Staffelkapitan knocked out the raft, but in fact the Oberleutnant's bombs destroyed the raft and Fuhrhop did not need to attack. Oberleutnant Hinrichs was awarded the Knight's Cross for his achievement, which played an important part in the destruction of the fortress. Bombers such as KG 51's Ju 88s were making four trips a day against Sevastopol, their crews staying aboard the aircraft while they were re-armed. This, coupled with the hot Crimean summer, the importance of accuracy, making every bomb count, and general ammunition shortages, added to the tensions which were building up within Luftwaffe bomber crews. There was no respite for them, for as soon as Sevastopol fell they were moved to support the offensive aimed at encircling the Russian 6th, 9th and 57th armies at Kharkov.

While this activity was going on, Goering had ample opportunity to demonstrate the efficiency of his transport units in providing aerial provisions. Over 100,000 troops had been encircled at Demyansk, a small town mid-way between Moscow and Leningrad. Six divisions of the German XVIth Army urgently needed help and this came in the form of the ungainly Ju 52, 40 of which began the airlift on February 20. There were two airfields in the besieged area and the heavily laden transports could only fly into them in daylight. By enlisting the help of training schools, collecting aircraft from every available source, and careful planning, the 300 tons of supplies needed daily to sustain the trapped men were delivered. In a similar situation at Kholm supplies were parachuted or landed by glider. The siege at Demyansk was lifted on May 18 and the men at Kholm held out for three months before they were relieved by ground forces. The airlift, although achieving its objectives, cost

the Luftwaffe over 300 transport aircraft and set a dangerous precedent.

The evidence pointed to a successful operation in which Goering had fulfilled all his promises, but one of the most salient points, which was conveniently overlooked, was that there had been little interference from the Soviet air force. In April 1942 improvements in the Mediterranean enabled more units to be moved back to the Russian front, thus bringing the total Luftwaffe establishment back to 2,750 combat aircraft.

In June an all-out offensive was mounted towards the River Don. Once again the familiar Blitzkrieg pattern was adopted with the Ju 87s and Hs 129s giving ground support, while the level bombers were engaged in attacking troop concentrations, lines of communications and fuel installations well behind the front line. The Russian army seemed to offer little resistance, preferring to trade ground for time, but at Stalingrad they halted and, with reinforcements pouring in, made a stand which has been recorded as being one of the most courageous and bloody battles of all time.

By mid-November the German army, which had been well supported by the bomber and dive-bomber units, had secured almost the whole of the western bank of the Volga; it looked as though the defenders would be hard pushed to hold on. But on the 19th of the month, a counter-attack was started outside the city whereby two Russian armies moving from the north and south carried out a pincer movement which trapped 22 divisions comprising some 300,000 men of the German VIth army. Generaloberst Friedrich Paulus could have attempted to break out and probably would have achieved his escape with acceptable casualties, but Hitler told him to stand firm and that his army would be supplied from the air. An army of this size needed supplies of food and ammunition totalling 600 tons a day. Most Luftwaffe field commanders in the area knew this figure was beyond the capability of the transport units. Despite their pleas to Paulus to get out while he could, the army commander stood firm, putting his trust in Goering's promises, which after all had been fulfilled at Demyansk.

To increase the number of aircraft available to support the Ju 52s the Luftwaffe was milked dry on every available front. He 111s of KG 55, two Gruppen of Ju 88s, and even one Gruppen of the ill-fated He 177 were taken off bombing duties to act as transport and alongside them operated Ju 86s, FW 200s, and Ju 290s. Despite the gallantry of the crews, their determination against fearful odds, and an enormous amount of work by ground crews, the required target of 600 tons a day was never reached, and gradually the VIth army was starved into submission. On February 2 Paulus surrendered the remains of his army (some 91,000 men), and the Luftwaffe took count of its losses. These totalled 488 aircraft, of which nearly 200 were bombers. Among these were seven of the new He 177s which had not even begun to operate in their designed role. From this time on, the writing was on the wall as far as the Russian campaign was concerned.

The Luftwaffe gradually became weaker both in replacement aircraft and crews and, although they continued to fight hard, the only real successes for the bomber force were achieved supporting the army. As more and more advanced Russian fighters began to be met in combat, losses rose at a remarkable rate. The training schools in Germany, already short of fuel, instructors, and operating severely curtailed programmes, were incapable of supplying enough replacements. In July 1943 Operation Zitadelle which was aimed at cutting off the Russian forces in Kursk was mounted, but by August it had failed. During this phase the Luftwaffe bomber units were seen for the last time in any strength, but once again it was mainly in a tactical role where they took heavy toll of Russian armour.

Increasing Allied bombing activity over Germany forced the withdrawal of a major proportion of the Luftwaffe left on the Eastern Front, especially as far as the Jagdgruppen were concerned. In December 1943 most of the medium bombers were also withdrawn from tactical support to mount a strategic offensive, but this never materialised in any great strength, and was far too late in the day to bring positive results. To balance the removal of bombers the ground attack units were strengthened and many of the Ju 87 Gruppen were replaced by FW 190F fighter bombers. These managed to stem the Russian advance for short periods but by January 1944 it was obvious that it was only a matter of time before not only the Luftwaffe but the whole German army in Russia was defeated.

As in every theatre, Luftwaffe bomber crews had fought valiantly with the equipment available. In 1941 this was clearly superior to anything the Russians had, but the failure of the Blitzkrieg technique to gain the success it had in other theatres should have brought a change in priority to a thorough strategic bombing campaign. The failure to do this, and hit at industry when the Russian air force was not capable of effectively defending it, possibly cost Germany the early victory she had hoped for. The continual demands for support on other fronts also resulted in the constant movement of units, which shows that despite its apparent strength at the opening of hostilities the Luftwaffe was not capable of supporting a multi-front campaign.

If the long-range so-called 'Ural bomber' had been proceeded with in 1938, or if the medium bombers had been used correctly, there may have been a different story to tell. But certainly none of the blame can be laid at the feet of the men who crewed the bombers whose gallantry and endeavour for their country would have been the same whatever equipment they had had to operate with.

ABOUT THE PHOTOGRAPHS

The photographs in this book have been selected with care from the Bundesarchiv, Koblenz (the approximate German equivalent of the US National Archives or the British Public Records Office). Particular attention has been devoted to choosing photographs which will be fresh to the majority of readers, although it is inevitable that one or two may be familiar. Other than this, the author's prime concern has been to choose good-quality photographs which illustrate the type of detail that enthusiasts and modellers require. In certain instances quality has, to a degree, been sacrificed in order to include a particularly interesting photograph. For the most part, however, the quality speaks for itself.

The Bundesarchiv files hold some one million black and white negatives of Wehrmacht and Luftwaffe subjects, including 150,000 on the Kriegsmarine, some 20,000 glass negatives from the inter-war period and several hundred colour photographs. Sheer numbers is one of the problems which makes the compilation of a book such as this difficult. Other difficulties include the fact that, in the vast majority of cases, the negatives have not been printed so the researcher is forced to look through box after box of 35 mm contact strips – some 250 boxes containing an average of over 5,000 pictures each, plus folders containing a further 115,000 contact prints of the Waffen-SS; moreover, cataloguing and indexing the negatives is neither an easy nor a short task, with the result that, at the present time, Luftwaffe and Wehrmacht subjects as well as entirely separate theatres of operations are intermingled in the same files.

There is a simple explanation for this confusion. The Bundesarchiv photographs were taken by war correspondents attached to German military units, and the negatives were originally stored in the Reich Propaganda Ministry in Berlin. Towards the close of World War 2, all the photographs – then numbering some $3\frac{1}{2}$ million – were ordered to be destroyed. One man in the Ministry, a Herr Evers, realised that they should be preserved for posterity and, acting entirely unofficially and on his own initiative, commandeered the first available suitable transport – two refrigerated fish trucks – loaded the negatives into them, and set out for safety. Unfortunately, one of the trucks disappeared en route and, to this day, nobody knows what happened to it. The remainder were captured by the Americans and shipped to Washington, where they remained for 20 years before the majority were returned to the government of West Germany. A large number, however, still reside in Washington. Thus the Bundesarchiv files are incomplete, with infuriating gaps for any researcher. Specifically, they end in the autumn of 1944, after Arnhem, and thus record none of the drama of the closing months of the war.

The photographs are currently housed in a modern office block in Koblenz, overlooking the River Mosel. The priceless negatives are stored in the basement, and there are strict security checks on anyone seeking admission to the Bildarchiv (Photo Archive). Regretably, and the author has been asked to stress this point, the archives are *only open to bona fide authors and publishers, and prints can only be supplied for reproduction in a book or magazine.* They CANNOT be supplied to private collectors or enthusiasts for personal use, so *please* – don't write to the Bundesarchiv or the publishers of this book asking for copy prints, because they cannot be provided. The well-equipped photo laboratory at the Bundesarchiv is only capable of handling some 80 to 100 prints per day because each is printed individually under strictly controlled conditions – another reason for the fine quality of the photographs but also a contributory factor in the above legislation.

THE
PHOTOGRAPHS

Previous page Dornier 17s returning from the opening sorties of Operation Barbarossa are filmed by a war correspondent (398/1756/5).

Above The business end of one of the Flak 18 37 mm cannons fitted to the Ju 87G (332/3100/15).

Left Ammunition for the 37 mm cannons. Each shell weighs 3 lb and is fitted with a high explosive head and has tremendous penetrative powers (332/3100/23).

Above right The clip of six 37 mm shells is about to be inserted into the cannon's magazine. There is much fine detail in this photograph for the fastidious modeller (332/3100/13).

Right The enormous size of the Ju 87 is very apparent in this view of a twin 37 mm cannon-armed Ju 87G-1 (332/3100/33a).

Left This Ju 87D-5 is coded S7 + AH and belongs to the 1st Staffel of I Gruppe StG 3. A hand-operated winch is being used to load the centre-line bomb on to its cradle. Note the aircraft's individual code letter painted on the undercarriage spat (726/224/26a).

Right The bleak Russian landscape indicates why the temporary white finish applied to Luftwaffe aircraft was so effective, even when it was becoming streaky and ready for replacement. The aircraft are Ju 87D-5s of StG 3 (726/224/3).

Below right Crank starting a Ju 87D-5 of I/StG 3. The underside of the wing tips and the rear fuselage band are yellow (726/223/6a).

Below A Ju 87D-3 of 2/StG 2. The temporary white winter camouflage has nearly worn away in several places and is a very good example of just how dirty this type of finish could become (393/1402/6a).

Top left The tank motif indicates a Panzerknacker of 10 (Pz)Sg 1, in other words, a Ju 87G-1 with two 37 mm cannon. Camouflage is Dunkelgrun overall on top surfaces and Hellblau under surfaces (353/1645/4).

Centre left This Ju 87D of StG 1 is coded A5 +KJ, which is a little unusual as 'J' was not often used for Stab, Gruppe or Staffel identification (461/221/3a).

Bottom left These two Ju 87Ds are very good examples of the scruffy condition which aircraft could get into when the winter camouflage started to show the effects of weather. The nearest aircraft is from the 2nd Staffel while the 'D' on the background machine indicates a Staff aircraft. Unit is not known (630/3558/28).

Right Aircraft of the 5th Staffel of II/StG 3 start a classic peel off at low level. The unit is probably rejoining the circuit pattern as all bombs have gone indicating either a successful mission or an unarmed training sortie (459/135/24).

Below The diving crow emblem on the nose of this Ju 87D belonged to I/StG 1 but was transferred to StG 3 whose code, S7, now appears forward of the cross. Full code is S7 + NP, indicating a II Gruppe aircraft. The horse-drawn wooden conveyance was used to carry bombs and large spare components (459/135/30).

Above T6 + GL, a Ju 87D-3 of II/StG 2, has been cleverly lined up by the photographer so that the winter sun is almost a reflection of the blank white disc painted on the cowling. Deliberate or accidental? Unfortunately we shall never know (630/3561/2a).

Below When the thaw brought mud conditions were probably more difficult. This Ju 87D-3 (S2 + NM) belongs to 4/II/StG 77 and has had its wheel covers removed, a not uncommon practice in such conditions (630/3562/20A).

Above A very loose formation of seven Ju 87Ds of StG 2 (634/3858/8).

Below There is much of interest in this view of a Ju 87D-1 of StG 2. The striped spinner is probably Schwarzgrun/yellow/white/Schwarzgrun, and the individual code letter 'L' on the spats is yellow outlined in black. The sirens on the undercarriage legs have their propellers fitted and the centre-line bomb cradle hangs empty (329/2984/5a).

Above The wing-mounted machine-guns and sirens have been removed from this Ju 87D-1, believed to belong to StG 77 and photographed in the southern sector of the eastern front in 1942 (634/3860/27).

Below A Staff aircraft of the III Gruppe of an unknown unit about to touch down in front of a very basic flying control unit. The flag gives the pilot visual indication of landing permission (667/7126/29).

Above right A variety of headgear and general dress is shown by these Luftwaffe groundcrew members carrying out final checks on a D-3 (503/183/30).

Below right Although this Ju 87D-5 carries the code of Lehrgeschwader 1, it is part of I/StG 5 and is having its wing racks loaded whilst a bomb-equipped FW 190A passes overhead (667/7103/24a).

Left The pilot of this Ju 87D-3 has been caught in the action of throwing back his shoulder straps. Note the map folded in the windscreen and the barrel of the wing-mounted MG 17 7.92 mm machine-gun (329/2984/6a).

Below This Ju 87D-8 has winter camouflage overall apart from the front sections of the undercarriage spats. It is likely these have been 'borrowed' from another machine as this aircraft's individual code is 'D' (459/132/5).

Above right The wave form camouflage pattern on this Ju 87D-8 appears to have been applied to the spinner and propeller as well as the main airframe. The underwing bomb is fitted with a Dienartstab percussion rod. The pilot just about to enter the cockpit is a Leutnant (665/6814/9).

Below right The famous Bonzo Dog badge of StG 2, which in this case has a blue background ringed in white, adorning the nose of a Ju 87D-2 of the Gruppenstab of I/StG 2 (454/1076/15).

Inset right The gunner of a Ju 87D-8. Tinted goggles were a must to combat the glare off the snow as well as direct sunlight. The rear sliding canopy, armour plating and internal structure is worthy of note (459/140/10).

Inset below right The Hs 126 carried out important reconnaissance work for the Luftwaffe and Wehrmacht. This one is picketed and has covers over its cockpit and engine. The aircraft landing is a Ju 87D-3 (655/6818/10a).

Inset left This ski-equipped Ju 87B/U4 makes interesting comparison with the normally seen wheeled variety. An interesting conversion subject for modellers (392/1334/7a).

Background photograph These four Ju 87D-3s have 70/71/65 camouflage, yellow rear fuselage bands and rudders, and names on the cowlings, the nearest being 'BERTHA'. Note the absence of wheel spats and the sirens (634/3857/20).

Above The outer bomb on this Ju 87D-8's wing rack has conventional fuzes but the inner one is fitted with a Dienartstab percussion rod. The rod seemingly fitted to the front of the outer bomb, is in fact the barrel of a wing-mounted MG 17 (459/140/11).

Left The moment of truth. A Ju 87D-5 of I/SG 5 peels off to start its dive. Code is L1 + CB. The dark area above the wing is shadow (460/176/3a).

Above right A fully armed Ju 87D-8 of I/SG 5 wings its way towards its target in the spring of 1944 (503/212/28).

Right Ju 87D-1s in 70/71/65 camouflage with the usual Eastern Front yellow fuselage bands and wing tips (454/ 1006/4).

Left The crew members of these Ju 87Ds are all wearing life jackets, which is a little unusual in most Russian Front situations. It is likely that a flight over or near the sea was to take place, or the target was a naval one. The nearest crew member is checking the sirens fitted to the bomb fins (634/3857/34a).

Below left this Ju 87D-5 takes on fuel prior to receiving its bomb load from the supply stacked in the snow (665/6818/30a).

Right The white winter camouflage was a water soluble paint sprayed over the normal camouflage. National markings and codes were not masked out and dark areas of the original finish often surround them. The Ju 87 in the background appears to have had its propeller blades sprayed white which seems to be carrying camouflage to extremes (665/6815/10a).

Below This is a very good illustration of a typical centre-line bomb and a Ju 87D-1 being prepared to receive it (634/3863/35a).

Inset right A 3 Staffel I Gruppe Ju 87D of an unknown unit which well illustrates the extremely crude winter finish camouflage and the areas where it was prone to wear away quickly (503/216/15a).

Inset below There does not appear to be any shortage of bombs for this Ju 87D of II Gruppe of an unknown unit (459/132/7).

Background photograph None of the 11 Ju 87Ds in this formation have their wheel spats fitted (634/3859/7a).

Above The crewman perched on a rather lethal seat in front of this D-3 appears to be really feeling the cold. The scattered bombs, boxes and equipment give a lot of scope for the diorama enthusiast (456/45/16).

Below This Ju 87D-1 is in pristine condition and is probably newly delivered. The fuel bowser has a rather interesting wave form camouflage (457/53/33a).

Above Protective covers over the wings, engine and cockpit keep out the harsh Russian winter. Aircraft is a D-3 (513/216/7).

Below 'Blackmen' use a form of three-wheeled trolley to take its load to a D-5. Note the absence of underwing dive brakes which were not fitted to all but a few early production models of this version (665/6818/20).

Inset above The machine-gun equipped nose of this Ju 88C-6a of 4/KG 76 has been painted to represent the glazed nose of the bomber version. These aircraft were used to attack road transport and troop concentrations. The badge on the nose is a goose wearing a British-style steel helmet, carrying an umbrella and smoking a cigar. A gunsight is superimposed over the motif (452/975/27).

Background photograph A classic shot of a Ju 88A-4 of I/KG 30. This extremely versatile aircraft was to the Luftwaffe what the Mosquito was to the RAF. It served on every front and in almost every role (638/4213/33).

Inset above The pilot of this Ju 88A-4 of I/KG 3 is a Hauptmann and he appears to be describing some problem to the engineering officer. The shield is white with red lightning. II Gruppe colours were reversed and III Gruppe had a yellow shield with red lightning (325/2782A/19).

Left The Leutnant celebrating his 700th mission is wearing a standard issue flying blouse carrying rank badges on the collar and shoulder. His gunner has a fur collar on his flight jacket but no rank badges. The pilot in the centre watching the proceedings is also a Leutnant and has a mission clasp above his left pocket, while the man to his left is an Oberfeldwebel and has a transport NCO badge on his left cuff (503/206/30).

Below left The wreckage of a Russian fighter makes a poignant setting for V4 + KN, a Ju 88A-5 of II/KG 1. Undersides of wing tips are yellow (389/1093/31).

Above right Another view of the train-busting Ju 88C-6a of KG 76's fourth Staffel (452/966/2a).

Centre right The fuselage of a Ju 88A-4 of I/KG 1 provides a rather precarious location for this group photograph. The heavily studded boots make one wince when the comparatively delicate airframe is considered. The aircraft belongs to the 2nd Staffel and its individual letter 'C' is outlined in (probably) red (330/3003/9a).

Right A II/KG 3 Ju 88A-4 with standard splinter camouflage. Code is 5K + FN (325/2780/10a).

Left A film cameraman records the celebrations as KG 3 celebrate their 30,000th sortie (325/2799/27a).

Below Ju 88A-4, WerK Nr 6689, code 5K + AS, belongs to the 8th Staffel of III/KG 3, and has splinter camouflage in two shades of green with light blue undersurfaces. The rear band is yellow and the individual letter 'A' is outlined in white (325/2782/31a).

Bottom The individual aircraft letter 'D' can be clearly seen under the starboard wing of this Ju 88A-4 of AuflGr 122. The winter camouflage is badly worn, especially on the engine nacelles (625/3191/16a).

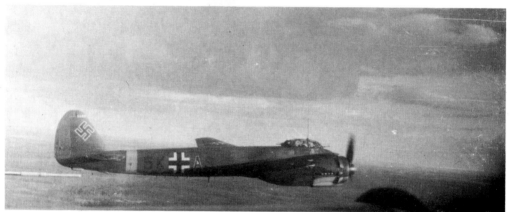

Above There is much of interest in this presentation of a Ju 88A-4 of I/AuflGr 22. The man on the right has the rank badge of a Major on his flying overalls and the officer to his left is a Leutnant. The position of the under-fuselage gondola entry hatch, and the size of the rear fuselage yellow band are worthy of note (329/2987/6a).

Below Starboard view of the same Ju 88. The individual code letter 'M' is red (329/2979/8).

Right Do 17Z-2 carrying the badge of 7/KG 3 on its nose. This badge was formerly that of III/KG 153 (449/786/5A).

Left This Heinkel He 111H-11 has modified nose armament consisting of two additional MG 131s under the MG FF mounted in the normal nose position (329/2989/16).

Left Aircraft of the 3rd (nearest) and 2nd Staffels of I/KG 3 formate en route to their target. The yellow fuselage band on the nearest aircraft has been painted well forward and makes interesting comparison with the position of the band on the following photograph (330/3010/5).

Below Exhaust stains have taken heavy toll of the white camouflage of this Ju 88A-4 of I/AuflGr 22, while the fin and rudder are also back to their original scheme (330/3001/18a).

Above Despite the sunshine the ground controller is well wrapped-up against the cold as he watches a ski-equipped Storch land over an He 111H-16 of I/KG 27. The disc propped against the small tree is yellow with a black L. It was used to indicate to an approaching pilot that there was a fault with his port undercarriage. If the starboard undercarriage was suspect then a yellow disc with a black R was used (327/2892/24).

Below This He 111H-20 has an MG 131 in the dorsal turret. It has a factory finish and was probably photographed in Poland in 1944. One undercarriage member has penetrated the top surface of the port wing. The small individual aircraft letter 'E' on the port wing is not commonly seen (666/6873/7a).

Above The He 111 was arguably the Luftwaffe's most successful medium bomber and was employed in this role throughout the war on every front. This is an He 111H-3 of 5/KG 27 photographed in April 1942 (326/2855/29a).

Right The fixed cupola in the dorsal position on the He 111 was eventually changed for a revolving turret as seen on this He 111H-21. A beam gun position can also be seen above and to the right of the canine flap inspector (462/229/22).

Below The fourth Staffel of KG 55 celebrates its 4,000th mission. The aircraft is an H-3 (498/1/13a).

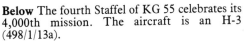

Above The unusual camouflage on the two lead aircraft of I/KG 27 leads to a lot of speculation. All three H-3s are carrying external bomb loads and have the familiar yellow fuselage bands and wing tips of Eastern Front aircraft (327/2879/21a).

Above right The engines of this He 111 are warmed prior to its being readied for a mission (78/21/6a).

Right Safely on the ground, this He 111 crew seem to be seeing the funny side of some minor battle damage (667/7133/25).

Left Protection against the weather was essential for man and machine. Two well clothed crewmen ensure that the He 111 also has its vulnerable parts protected (503/218/16a).

Left This He 111 is rather unusual in that it was one of 30 H-8/R2 versions originally fitted with cable cutting equipment around the wings and nose. This gear has now been removed and the aircraft is serving as a glider tug with I/SchleppGruppe 4, whose badge can be seen below the cockpit (331/3026/2).

Below left Overalls, fur-lined boots and long greatcoats are the order of the day for this refuelling crew as they replenish an aircraft of KG 27 (327/2892/14).

Top right In the event of a wheels-up landing the He 111 pilot could elevate his seat to get a better view, and in this position was protected by a small screen. The open hatch and screen can be clearly seen in this photograph. The crew's expression requires no further comment (667/7134/13).

Centre right An H-16 of an unknown unit awaits take-off clearance. The rudder is yellow and the area aft of the fuselage cross appears to have been cleaned off to accept new codes (328/2907/30a).

Right It is likely that this photograph was not taken on the Russian front although it is in the Bundesarchiv files for that area. It is included as it gives a good impression of the one-piece flying suit worn by bomber crews (325/2777a/32).

Above A hand-operated fuelling pump stands sentinel over this H-16 whose fuselage bomb bay is open ready to accept the siren-equipped bombs (327/2892/23).

Below The MG FF 20 mm cannon fitted to the nose positions of the He 111 from the H-3 version onwards. Variations can be seen on all models (634/3883/7a).

Above Hot air is blown around the engines of this He 111H-16 which has its individual code letter painted inboard of the landing light. The Klemm trainer in the background was probably used for communication work (503/221/36a).

Below The modified dorsal gun cupola of the H-16 which was first used on the H-11 improved the gunner's comfort and was greatly appreciated by those who had operated in the earlier open-ended cupolas (640/4493/17a).

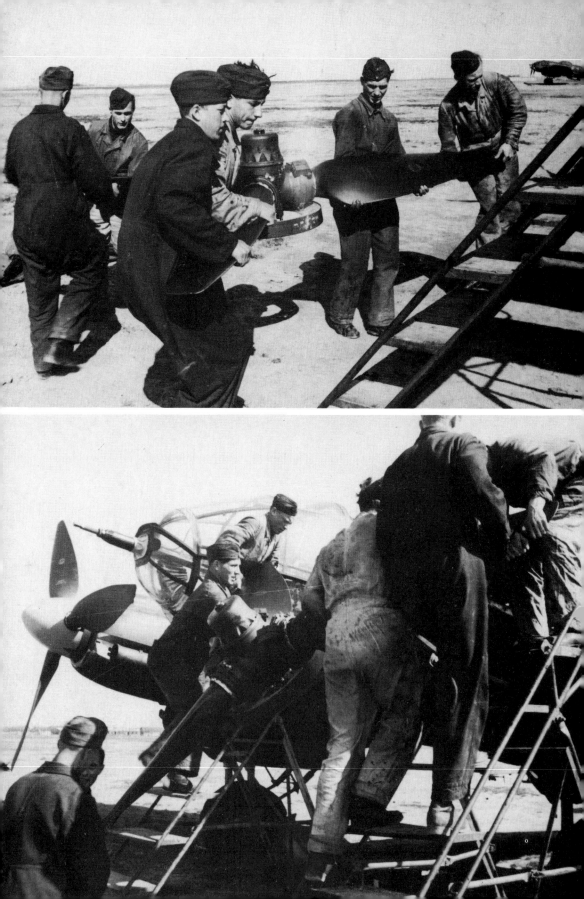

Left Six men, two ladders and a lot of care were required to change the propeller of an He 111 (636/4051/2a and 3a).

Above The modified exhaust stacks, dorsal turret and nose armament of the late H-20 series marks of the ubiquitous He 111 are all apparent in this wintery scene (503/221/33a).

Below The undersurfaces of this H-16 have been daubed with black paint as have the white areas of the fuselage cross (636/4068/23).

An unknown Luftwaffe General visits the Eastern Front in 1943. Aircraft is an He 111H-11 and has factory codes as well as a new finish which is 71 on upper surfaces and 65 on lower (460/193/7 and 9).

Above An He 111H 1G + IH
of 1/KG 27 and a Bf 110E of ZG
1 with an FW 190 and a Storch
(wing tip beneath nose of He
111) make a representative
quartet of Russian Front aircraft (630/3568/31a).

Left This aircraft and much
decorated crew, of which one
member has spectacles, is
believed to belong to KG 27.
Nose armament has been
removed and the plate fitted
gives every indication of this
being a permanent arrangement
(674/7794/13a).

Right The strain on the Oberfeldwebel's face and the intent
concentration of the man in the
white winter hat, would appear
to indicate that there is quite a
story behind the battle damage
to the aircraft's trailing edge.
K7 was the code for Nachtauf-
laerungsgruppe (329/2985/12).

Above left He 111H-11 with black under-surface centre section which contrasts with the white winter camouflage, yellow wing tips and fuselage band. The remainder of the under-surfaces appear to be Hellblau. (327/2879/2a).

Centre left A clean and tidy H-11 of KG 27 in overall 71 and 65 (325/2776a/33a).

Below left The five-man crew of a KG 27 He 111 show off their winter flying clothing (327/2879/4a).

Above A KG 27 crewman wearing a chest type parachute harness makes use of a wooden bomb case to study his flight plan before boarding his aircraft. The képi was popular with both air and ground crews (327/2895/8).

Above right The external fuselage bomb load of this He 111H can be clearly seen in this familiar air-to-air pose (325/2776a/16).

Below right Once again the rather unusual black centre-section and leading edge camouflage is prominent in this view of a KG 27 aircraft (327/2895/17).

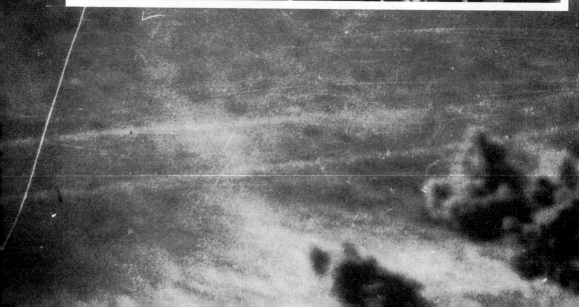

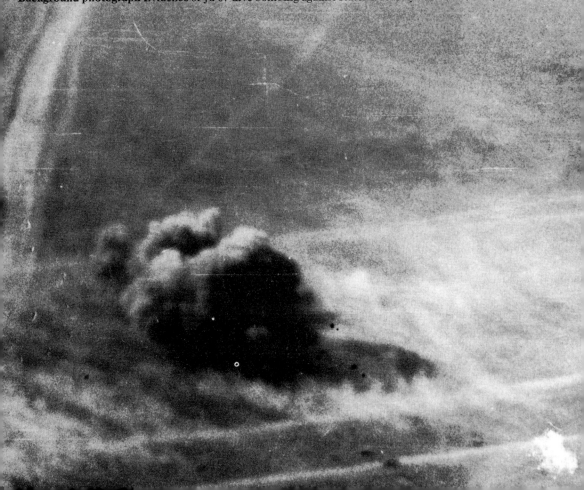

Inset above Pilot's view from an He 111 (325/2777a/27).
Inset above left Radio operator/rear gunner of a Ju 88A-4 (325/2789/25a).
Inset below left Pilot and observer in the cockpit of a Ju 88A-4 (324/2789/27a).
Background photograph Evidence of Ju 87 dive bombing against Russian road systems (454/1076/34).

Above Pilot, observer, and engineer/gunner of an He 111 (460/200/6).

Below Tinted goggles are a must for this crew and the gloved hands indicate that even in the extensively glazed nose of the He 111, cold could be a problem (499/60/38).

Right The radio operator of a Ju 88. His rank is Oberfeldwebel and is indicated by the badge on the sleeve of his flying suit. The butt of one of the two MG 81 rear defensive guns can be seen above the radio (388/954/25a).

Above Russian propaganda sources released this photograph of a Ju 88A-4 believed to have been from 1/AuflGr 122 which was shot down by ground fire. It was reproduced in the western press with the headline shown (unnumbered print).

Below Gunner's view from the rear cockpit of a Ju 87 as it pulls out of its bombing dive (454/1057/14).

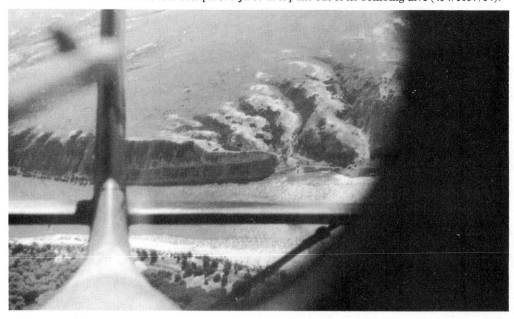

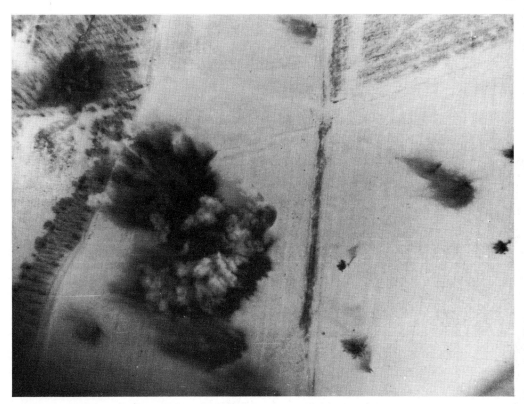

Above Bombs from a Ju 87 explode to the left of the target which is the road, craters to the right indicate earlier near misses (503/206/24a).
Below The snow has melted but the thaw brings no respite to Russian armour which is attacked by fighter-bombers and dive bombers whenever it appears (454/1057/19).

Above and below Railways came in for just as much attention as other communication systems. These photographs were taken from He 111s attacking such a target (498/27/38 and 498/28/15).

Right One Ju 87 has left its mark on the road, and a second is about to commence its dive (503/207/15a).

Inset right 20 mm ammunition for the wing gun of an FW 190. Every third shell is an armour-piercing one and the others are tracers (457/53/34a).

Left This Unteroffizer has a back-type parachute, leather flight blouse and a one-piece flying suit. His goggles are of the tinted type as worn by the observer (197/1248/19).

Below An Hs 126 of AuflGr 21 which has had its wheel spats removed; a common practice on both this aircraft and the Ju 87. Fuselage band is yellow, top surfaces are two-tone splinter green, and under-surface blue (325/2782a/27).

Above right The extreme cold took a severe toll of men and aircraft. It was essential that both were protected by covers and warm clothing, and on some occasions ground crews started engines throughout the cold nights to stop lubricants freezing. These two Hs 126s have protective tents over their engines to give some form of cover to crews working on them (353/1615/22A).

Below right Bombers supporting the army cannot operate without good reconnaissance back-up; the Hs 126 was used extensively for this and in this picture an Oberleutnant briefs the crew of such an aircraft while a mechanic carries out a final check (209/69/9a).

These photographs typify the clothing and equipment so necessary in the Russian winter. The Hs 126 belongs to AuflGr 32 and is picketed against the wind by wooden crates tied to its wing struts. An ordinary domestic broom is being used to remove the snow, and the unit providing hot air for the engine is fitted to a sleigh (353/1615/16a and 15a and 353/1613/18a).

Left and below This Bf 110G-2 belongs to Stab/SKG 210 which was formed in 1941 from ZG 1 for the invasion of Russia. The famous Wespen insignia was retained and used on Bf 110s by ZG 1 and SKG 210, the latter once again became renamed ZG 1 in 1942 before it left Russia for the Mediterranean front (630/3562/35a and 33a).

Right Bombs being loaded by means of a small hand-operated hydraulic winch on to the ETC 500 fuselage rack of a Bf 110E-2 of SKG 210 (620/3568/38A).

Below right A Bf 110E-2 of ZG 26 with flaps down and engines throttled back, makes its final approach to a very wet landing ground (389/1072/5).

Above A destroyed MiG 3 is examined by Luftwaffe personnel. In the background can be seen a Polikarpov I-15 (389/1060

Right The bombers didn't always have it their own way. The wing of this Ju 87 shows considerable damage from ground fire (353/1638/8A).

Below The tailplane of this winter-camouflaged Hs 126 has been damaged by the nearby explosion of a 76 mm anti-aircraft shell (143/1377/29a).

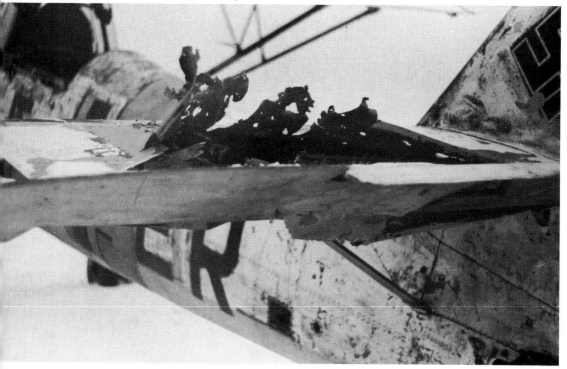

Above An FW 190A4/U3 about to receive its SC 250 (550 lb) bomb. The ribbon hanging from the undercarriage leg shows that a ground locking pin is still in place and must be removed before flight (634/3874/26A).

Right Fighter bombers were used to harrass enemy troops and armour. This FW 190A4/U3 has a single SC 250 bomb on its centre-line rack (634/3874/32A).

Below Interesting detail of a 550 lb bomb on the ETC rack of an FW 190A4. The bar which appears to be hanging just behind the port trailing edge is the retractable step into the cockpit (464/381/37).

Left When the snow came it was not always necessary to produce man-made camouflage; but even the natural sort has to be removed and a start has just been made on this KG 3 Do 17Z-2 (449/778/18a).

Below left A KG 3 Do 17Z-2 in the process of being camouflaged against aerial reconnaissance. The first-aid box position by the code '5' and the aerials under the fuselage are all useful modelling details (449/769/27).

Right This Do 17P-1 was used for reconnaissance for a very short time at the beginning of Operation Barbarossa. The blue shield is edged in white and has a yellow moon and stars on it, the telescope is black and the choirboy wears a white surplice (410/1079/17).

Below The Bf 109 was also used in the fighter-bomber role as illustrated by these two G6/R1 versions in winter camouflage. Markings on the nearest aircraft indicate the Geschwader Adjutant's aircraft, and those in the background the aircraft of the Gruppen Kommanduer (667/7126/22A).

Prior to the Russian campaign the Luftwaffe experienced wintery conditions in Norway and Poland. This Do 17P-1 belonged to a communication Staffel in Norway and has a badge consisting of an orange sun rising from a pale blue sea on a background of a Balkankreuz. No doubt those who experienced conditions in Norway did not find Russia as bad as those who had not already had to cope with snow, frozen limbs and aircraft (353/1612/12, 22 and 23).

Left Forerunner in the dive bombing role was the biplane Hs 123, which saw some service on the Eastern Front. This is the aircraft of Leutnant Josef Menapace of II/SG 2. The infantry support badge can be seen aft on the cowling (454/1071/36).

Below left The Do 17Z-2, as depicted by this aircraft of KG 2 taken on a Balkans airfield in early 1941, bore the brunt with the He 111 of the early bombing of Russian military targets in June 1941 (534/27/8).

Right Good example of the early style bomber crew life jacket and flying helmet (561/1140/15).

Below Do 17Ps like this one photographed in Poland were used in small quantities by the Luftwaffe in the opening phase of the Russian campaign (724/149/15).

Left This Ju 88 crewman has the familiar light brown one-piece flying suit, winter flying helmet and leather belt with holster (325/2780/33A).

Below This rather unusual load for a He 111 seems to be some form of container for bombs and/or ammunition, although the stencilling might well be a legacy from a previous usage (667/7133/3).

Right The interesting gun arrangement, open hatches and crew access ladder are points that come over well in this view of an FW 189A-2 of 1(H)/32 (330/3015/18).

Below right Airfields were protected against intrusion by Russian fighter bombers and bombers by anti-aircraft guns such as this quad 20 mm Flakvierling. Aircraft is an He 111H of KG 27 (329/2978/11).

Inset left This Hs 129B-2 of II/SG 2 has two tank kills on its rudder and its Werk Nr, 0508, painted in white on the fin. Fuselage band is yellow as are the tips of the spinners. The 'box' in front of the windscreen is the gun sight (636/4076/32).

Background photograph Another KG 100 He 177A-3/R2 similar to the type used in Russia. The large size of the aircraft can be appreciated by the crewmen perched on the fuselage (668/7161/30A).

Inset right The ill-fated He 177 was used in small numbers in Russia by 8/KG 1. The aircraft was even used to drop supplies to beleaguered troops at Stalingrad during which seven were lost. This example is a KG 100 machine which was similar to the He 177A-5 used in Russia (461/220/7).

Above Primarily used for reconnaissance, and much preferred purely because of its creature comforts over the Hs 126, the FW 189A-2 could carry a small bomb load on wing racks which are empty on this occasion (725/179/26A).

Below Sirens are attached to the fins of the 110 lb bomb being loaded on to the outer rack of this 2(H) 31 FW 189A. The badge on the engine cowling indicates that the aircraft is attached to a Panzer unit and has a black tank on a red background with a white stylised cloud coming from the turret (331/3034/13A).

Above In the ground-attack role the pugnacious looking Hs 129B-2 had few equals. This is a B-2/R2 version of IV(Pz)/SG 9, which was part of the VIII Fliegerkorps, and was photographed at Czernovitz (503/231/14).

Below Cannon shells for the 30mm MK 103 under-fuselage weapon of the Hs 129B-2/R2. This weapon was devastating against tanks and AFVs (503/231/23A).

Above The He 177 could have provided the Luftwaffe with a sound strategic bomber if it had not become a pawn in political infighting. These four armourers attend to the bomb load of a KG 100 aircraft on the Western Front (496/3500/8).

Below Russian fighters were no match for the Luftwaffe in the opening days of the campaign. This Polikarpov I-16 type 10 is typical of the opposition offered by the Red Air Force (212/224/26A).

Above Blue 'N', an Hs 129B-2 of 8(Pz)II/SG 2 in September 1943. The Werk Nr is painted in white on the fin (0373) and camouflage is two-tone green splinter and blue under-surfaces (333/3104/38A).

Below The stalwart workhorse of the Luftwaffe's transport arm was the ever-reliable Ju 52. The badge on the nose has been attributed to a blind flying school; however, other evidence (see number 7 in this series) suggests strongly that it may belong to a Fallschirmjäger unit instead (538/331/16).

Left The 7·92 mm dorsal-mounted MG 15 looks a little incongruous against the red crosses on this Ju 52/3m g63 (513/223/5A).

Below left The familiar corrugated skin, exposed engine, simple D/F loop and primitive but effective door opening, all capture the homely air of this classic aircraft (503/223/2A).

Above As well as carrying troops, fuel and equipment the Ju 52, affectionately known as 'Tante Ju', was an airborne ambulance. This 3m g6e has the familiar red crosses in place of its national markings and yellow wing tips (503/223/6A).

Below Casualty evacuation of all injured personnel was in the hands of either the enormous Me 323 Gigant or the Ju 52. One of the former is being loaded under very wintery conditions (503/223/36A).

APPENDICES

1. Bomber and associate units and their aircraft available at the opening of the Russian campaign on June 22 1941

Luftflotte 2

Recce Gruppe (F)/122	Ju 88
KG 3	Ju 88
KG 53	He 111H2–6
StG 77	Ju 87
KG 102 (transport unit)	Ju 52

Luftflotte 4

Recce Gruppe 4(F)/122	Ju 88
KG 50 (transport unit)	Ju 52
KG 54 (transport unit)	Ju 52
KG 51	Ju 88
KG 54	Ju 88
KG 55	He 111H2–6
4(F)/121	Ju 88
KG 27	He 111
3(F)/121	Ju 88

Luftflotte 1

Recce Gruppe 2(F)Ob.d.L	Do 215
KG 106 (transport unit)	Ju 52
KG 1	Ju 88
KG 76	Ju 88
KG 77	Ju 88
Recce Gruppe 5(F)/122	Ju 88

Luftflotte 5

KG 106 (transport unit)	Ju 52
KG 30	Ju 88
St/LG 1	Ju 87
1(F)120	Ju 88

2. Luftwaffe aircraft on Russian front as a percentage of total aircraft available to all fronts:

	Total	%
June 1941	2,770	64
December 1941	2,500	58
December 1942	2,450	62
August 1943	1,750	37
June 1944	2,085	45

3. Aircraft used in bombing roles in Russia

Ju 87D

Span:	45 feet $3\frac{1}{4}$ inches. Length: 36 feet 5 inches.
Engine:	Jumo 211J liquid-cooled 12-cylinder inverted V.
Bomb load:	3,968 lb.
Armament:	Pair of wing-mounted MG 17 and two 7·92 mm MG 15 in rear cockpit.

Henschel 129B–1

Span:	46 feet 7 inches. Length: 31 feet $11\frac{3}{4}$ inches.
Engines:	Two 690 hp Gnome-Rhône two row 14-cylinder air-cooled radials.
Bomb load:	240 lb or 48 fragmentation bombs.
Armament:	Two 7·9 mm MG 17 and two 20 mm MG 151 cannon.

Henschel 123

Span:	34 feet $5\frac{1}{2}$ inches. Length: 27 feet 4 inches.
Engine:	880 hp BMW 132D nine-cylinder air-cooled radial.
Bomb load:	Four 110 lb bombs on underwing racks or clusters of anti-personnel fragmentation bombs.
Armament:	Two 7·92 mm MG 17 mounted in engine cowling and firing through propeller arc.

Heinkel He 111H–3

Span:	74 feet $1\frac{3}{4}$ inches. Length: 53 feet $9\frac{1}{2}$ inches.
Engines:	Two 1,200 hp Jumo 211D–2, inverted V, 12-cylinder liquid-cooled.
Bomb load:	4,410 lb.
Armament:	Three 7·92 mm MG 15 in nose, dorsal and gondola positions, plus two MG 15 or MG 17 in waist windows, and one similar fixed firing forward; also one 20 mm cannon in nose section of gondola. Armament could vary depending on field conditions.

Other titles in the same series

No 1 Panzers in the desert
by Bruce Quarrie

No 2 German bombers over England
by Bryan Philpott

No 3 Waffen-SS in Russia
by Bruce Quarrie

No 4 Fighters defending the Reich
by Bryan Philpott

No 5 Panzers in North-West Europe
by Bruce Quarrie

No 6 German fighters over the Med
by Bryan Philpott

No 7 German paratroops in the Med
by Bruce Quarrie

In preparation

No 9 Panzers in Russia 1941-43
by Bruce Quarrie

No 10 German fighters over England
by Bryan Philpott

No 11 U-Boats in the Atlantic
by Paul Beaver

No 12 Panzers in Russia 1943-45
by Bruce Quarrie

Plus many more!